Animals and Plants

Harcourt

SCHOOL PUBLISHERS

Orlando   Austin   New York   San Diego   Toronto   London

Visit *The Learning Site!*

www.harcourtschool.com

Environment and Adaptations

Do you know what an **environment** is? It is made up of all the things in a place. It has living things, such as plants and animals. It has nonliving things, such as rocks and water.

This environment has fish in it. There are rocks and plants in it, too.

This bush tastes bad to the animals that want to eat it. This is an adaptation that helps it live.

An **adaptation** is a body part or behavior that helps a living thing.

Some plants have adaptations. Thorns on blackberries stop animals from eating them. Waxy coverings on desert cactus plants help them store water.

 MAIN IDEA AND DETAILS Water in a pond is nonliving. A fish in the same pond is living. Are they part of the same environment? Why?

3

Animals Have Adaptations

Animals have adaptations, too. Some adaptations make eating easy. A strong beak helps a woodpecker find food in a tree.

Some adaptations help animals move. Webbed feet help ducks swim.

Fish have scales that bend. The scales help fish move through water.

The lizard looks like the branch it is on. This is camouflage.

Some adaptations keep animals safe. Sharp quills on a porcupine keep other animals away.

Some adaptations help animals stay safe or find food. **Camouflage** is an animal's color or pattern that helps it hide.

Fast Fact

Sharks have an adaptation called gills. Gills allow sharks and other fish to breathe underwater.

COMPARE AND CONTRAST How are a fish's scales like duck's feet?

Animals Help Plants

Plants and animals need each other. Bees carry pollen from one flower to another. **Pollen** is a powder that flowers need to make seeds. Pollen helps plants make new plants. Plants need bees.

Bees like purple, blue, and yellow flowers best.

Fast Fact

Bees buzz, but they are not talking. Their wings move back and forth very fast. That makes the buzzing sound that we hear.

Sometimes animals carry seeds in their fur. They take the seeds to new places. Bears, foxes, and wolves carry seeds like this. Then these seeds can grow into new plants.

 SEQUENCE What can happen to a seed after a wolf carries it away from a plant?

Burrs from plants stick to this fox's fur as it walks. The burrs drop off and new plants grow.

Plants Help Animals

Plants help animals in many ways. Animals use plants to make homes. A bird makes a nest from leaves and twigs.

Animals can also hide in plants. Some snakes climb trees and hide there.

This nest took time to build. The bird used different kinds of plants.

This caterpillar was hungry!

Some animals use plants for food. Caterpillars eat leaves. Cows eat corn.

Oxygen is a kind of gas that is in air. Animals need to breathe oxygen to live. Plants give off oxygen.

 MAIN IDEA AND DETAILS What do plants do to help animals breathe?

Fast Fact

The largest bird's nest was built by bald eagles in Florida. It was 9 feet 6 inches (2.9 meters) wide and 20 feet (6 meters) deep.

Animals Help Animals

Animals need other animals, too. Some young animals need their parents. Some parents feed their young. Some parents keep their young safe.

This kangaroo keeps her young safe in her pouch.

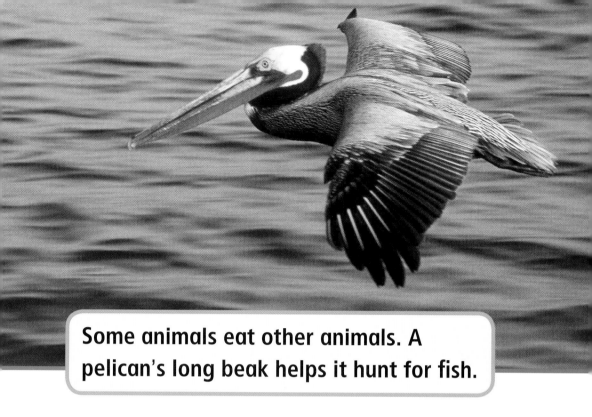

Some animals eat other animals. A pelican's long beak helps it hunt for fish.

 MAIN IDEA AND DETAILS How do some parents help their young after they are born?

Summary

Plants and animals have adaptations. Their adaptations help them live in their environments. Plants help animals. Animals help plants. Animals help other animals, too.

Glossary

adaptation A body part or behavior that helps a living thing (3, 4, 5, 11)

camouflage A kind of adaptation where an animal's color or pattern helps it hide (5, 11)

environment All the things that are in a place (2, 3, 11)

oxygen A kind of gas that plants give off and animals need to breathe (9)

pollen A powder that flowers need to make seeds (6)